# Puss in Boots and Kitty

by Katie Woolley and Valentina Bandera

## FRANKLIN WATTS
LONDON•SYDNEY

Once, there was a miller. He had three sons. Before the miller died, he gave his mill to his eldest son. He gave his donkey to his middle son.

The miller gave his two cats
to his youngest son.

"I have no money to look after
these cats!" said the youngest son.

"I must go and seek my fortune!"

Puss was not a clever cat,

but he could talk to humans.

Kitty could not talk to humans,

but she was clever!

"We need to make our master rich,"

Kitty told Puss. "Ask him to get us

some boots."

Puss asked his master to buy
two pairs of boots. The miller's son
was very surprised to hear his cat talk.
But he got the cats some boots.

The next day, Kitty put some lettuce in a bag. She left the bag next to a rabbit's burrow.
It wasn't long before a rabbit hopped into the bag.

Kitty trapped the rabbit and took it

back to Puss.

"I have a plan," said Kitty.

"We are going to pretend that

our master is the Lord of Carrabas.

You must do everything I tell you."

Puss and Kitty took the bag to the king. "Tell the king that this rabbit is a gift from our master, the Lord of Carrabas," said Kitty.

And Puss did what he was told.

He pretended that the rabbit was a gift from their master, the Lord of Carrabas.

The next day, Kitty had another plan. "The king will be passing the river in his carriage today. Tell our master to wash in the river," she told Puss.

When their master went to wash

in the river, Kitty hid his clothes.

Soon, the king's carriage came past.

"Quick!" Kitty told Puss.

"Tell the king that someone has taken our master's clothes."

And Puss did what he was told.

The king and his daughter wanted
to help. They sent for some clothes
for the Lord of Carrabas and said
they would take him home
in their carriage.

On the way, they came to

a beautiful castle.

Kitty had another plan.

She and Puss ran up to the castle.

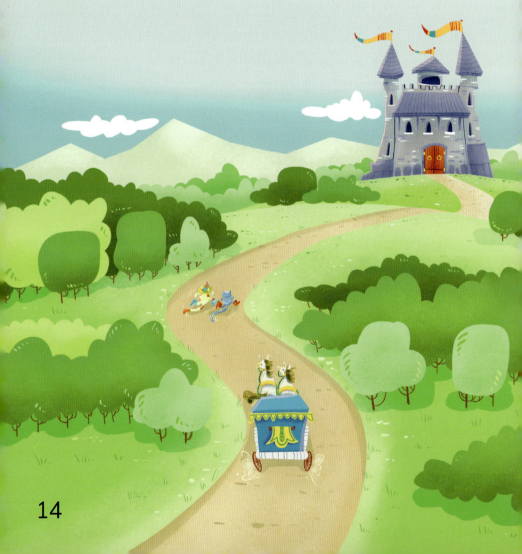

They knocked on the castle door.
Kitty knew that a terrible giant lived
there, and this giant could turn into
any animal he wanted.

"Oh, wonderful giant!" Kitty said
to the giant. "I hear you can turn into
any animal you want!"
The giant laughed and turned
into a lion.

"Very clever!" said Kitty. "Can you turn into something small, like a mouse?"
"Of course!" laughed the giant.
He turned into a mouse,
and Puss gobbled him up.

Kitty told Puss to pretend this was their master's castle. And he did.

The miller's son was very surprised.

The king liked the castle.

His daughter liked the Lord of Carrabas.

The next day, the king's daughter married the Lord of Carrabas. And they lived happily ever after with their two cats.

# Story order

Look at these 5 pictures and captions.
Put the pictures in the right order
to retell the story.

**1**

The miller's son rode in the king's carriage.

**2**

Puss said the castle belonged to his master.

**3**

The giant turned into a lion.

**4**

The miller's son gave his cats some boots.

**5**

Kitty hid the miller's son's clothes.

# Independent Reading

This series is designed to provide an opportunity for your child to read on their own. These notes are written for you to help your child choose a book and to read it independently.

In school, your child's teacher will often be using reading books which have been banded to support the process of learning to read. Use the book band colour your child is reading in school to help you make a good choice. *Puss in Boots and Kitty* is a good choice for children reading at Turquoise Band in their classroom to read independently. The aim of independent reading is to read this book with ease, so that your child enjoys the story and relates it to their own experiences.

## About the book
The miller gives his youngest son two cats. One can talk to humans; the other is very clever! Puss and Kitty want the miller's son to be rich ...

## Before reading
Help your child to learn how to make good choices by asking: "Why did you choose this book? Why do you think you will enjoy it?" Look at the cover together and ask: "What do you think the story will be about?" Support your child to think of what they already know about the story context. Read the title aloud and ask: "What is unusual about the cats?" Remind your child that they can try to sound out the letters to make a word if they get stuck.

Decide together whether your child will read the story independently or read it aloud to you.

## During reading

If reading aloud, support your child if they hesitate or ask for help by telling them the word. Remind your child of what they know and what they can do independently. If reading to themselves, remind your child that they can come and ask for your help if stuck.

## After reading

Support comprehension by asking your child to tell you about the story. Use the story order puzzle to encourage your child to retell the story in the right sequence, in their own words. The correct sequence can be found on the next page.
Give your child a chance to respond to the story: "Did you have a favourite part? Did you expect the miller's son to become rich?" Help your child think about the messages in the book that go beyond the story and ask: "Why was the miller's son so surprised when he arrived at the giant's castle? How does he feel at the end of the story?"

## Extending learning

Think about the story with your child, and make comparisons with the story *Puss in Boots*, if this story is known to them. Help your child understand the story structure by using the same story context and adding different elements. "Let's make up a new story about clever pets helping their owners. What happens in your story?"
In the classroom, your child's teacher may be reinforcing punctuation. On a few of the pages, ask your child to find the speech marks that show us where someone is talking and then read it aloud, making it sound like talking. Find the exclamation marks and ask your child to practise the expression they use for these.

Franklin Watts
First published in Great Britain in 2024
by Hodder and Stoughton
Copyright © Hodder and Stoughton, 2024

Series Editors: Jackie Hamley and Melanie Palmer
Series Advisors: Dr Sue Bodman and Glen Franklin
Series Designers: Cathryn Gilbert and Peter Scoulding

A CIP catalogue record for this book is
available from the British Library.

ISBN 978 1 4451 8955 0 (hbk)
ISBN 978 1 4451 8957 4 (pbk)
ISBN 978 1 4451 8956 7 (ebook)


Printed in China

Franklin Watts
An imprint of
Hachette Children's Group
Part of Hodder and Stoughton
Carmelite House
50 Victoria Embankment
London EC4Y 0DZ

An Hachette UK Company
www.hachette.co.uk

www.reading-champion.co.uk

Answer to Story order: 4, 5, 1, 3, 2